PRISON F

CW00546036

PRISON POEMS

by

Mahvash Sabet

Adapted from the original Persian
by
Bahiyyih Nakhjavani

Based on translations
by
Violette and Ali Nakhjavani

GEORGE RONALD
OXFORD

George Ronald, Publisher, Ltd.
Oxford
www.grbooks.com

Reprinted 2015, 2017

A catalogue record for this book is
available from the British Library

ISBN 978-0-85398-569-3

Cover design: Steiner Graphics

Contents

*This book is dedicated
to the noble members of the Yaran,
to the Bahá'ís of Iran,
and to all those who have been suffering so unjustly
in its prisons over the past decades*

Foreword

*Member of the Center of Human Rights Defenders and
one of the four lawyers for the Yaran*

Mahvash Sabet is a member of the Bahá'í community of Iran. She served for the past several years as secretary of an informal council of seven individuals known as the Yaran, who have been responsible for managing the affairs of the Iranian Bahá'í community. She was born in 1953, in the province of Ardestan, but grew up in Tehran and is the mother of two children as well as a university graduate in psychology. Prior to the Revolution, Mahvash was a teacher and subsequently a principal at a number of schools; she was also a trained psychologist and worked closely in this capacity with the National Literacy Committee of Iran. After the establishment of the Islamic Republic, she was expelled from her position and was permanently barred from all teaching posts connected with the State. For the next fifteen years, she was involved in running the Bahá'í Institute for Higher Education, which provided alternative educational opportunities for Bahá'í youth who had been denied access to universities by the State.

On 5 March 2008, Mahvash Sabet was arrested in Mashhad by representatives of the Ministry of Intelligence and National Security. She was later transferred to the security section of the detention centre of Evin in Tehran where the six other members of the Yaran soon joined her, after early morning raids on their homes on 14 May. Like them, she was jailed for two-and-a-half years without a proper hearing, and kept both in solitary confinement and with her companion Fariba Kamalabadi, in the penitentiaries of Evin, Ghohardasht, and Gharchak. She was also subjected, with them, to trials on 12 January, 7 February and 12 April 2010, each of which was aborted because of constitutional irregularities. She was finally convicted and condemned, as they were, to twenty years imprisonment on 12 June 2010. But she has in fact been detained longer than all of them so far.

When I accepted to defend the Bahá'í prisoners, together with Shirin Ebadi, Abdul-Fattah Soltani and Hadi Ismail-Zadih, I had not yet met any members of the Yaran personally. None of them had had access to legal counsel when Tehran's Security Court announced, on 11 February 2009, that they were accused of spying for Israel and of blasphemous propaganda against the Islamic Republic. My first encounter with Mahvash Sabet took place on a hot summer's day that same year, in Evin. After many hours of tedious waiting in a special room set aside for lawyers, I was finally allowed to meet her in the presence of two women guards. She was handcuffed to her companion Fariba, and although they said nothing themselves, it was obvious from the colour of their skin that the Bahá'í prisoners had been deprived of fresh air and daylight for a long time; their entire beings seemed thirsty for the energizing heat and light of the sun. However, despite all their hardships, their will remained unbroken and they were determined to give up their lives, if necessary, for their beliefs.

Although the Bahá'í community had come into existence in Iran some 168 years before she was even born, the first charge against Mahvash was that she was responsible for the formation of an illegal organization that aimed at the subversion of state security. This was followed by other accusations, including her role as secretary of the Yaran, espionage activities for Israel, the illegal promotion of the Bahá'í Faith and the desire to undermine the Islamic regime. This was the sum total of the charges levelled against her.

A study of the file showed that the grounds on which the Ministry of Intelligence had come to this conclusion were based on nothing more than the prisoners' adherence to the Bahá'í Faith. However, since the Constitution of the Islamic Republic prohibits inquiry or investigation into peoples' beliefs, political motives had to be invented in order to justify the arrest of the Yaran and their indictment on grounds of illegal activity. In fact the Ministry of Intelligence and the judicial powers were trying to evade the law; they were evoking political motives as a cover-up for their unconstitutional actions. And it was on this basis that these people were arrested and finally condemned to twenty years in jail.

In addition, the prosecution took advantage of a *fatwa* or religious decree by Ayatullah Makarem Shirazi issued in July 2009 stating that the Bahá'ís were warring against God and spreading corruption on the earth. But beneath all these false accusations there was nothing more than their belief in their Faith and their commitment to running the affairs of the Bahá'í community.

The trial of Mahvash and her co-workers officially began on 12 January 2010, in Branch 28 of the Revolutionary Court in Tehran. The presiding judge, who was dressed in clerical robes, was called Maqiseh. Throughout the proceedings Mahvash was firm and determined, brave and dignified; she seemed fearless of the outcome of the court's decision against her. Her principal concern was for the Bahá'í community in Iran. She believed that it was not herself but her Faith and those who believed in it that were on trial. No matter how severe the retribution it might incur, she repeatedly stated that the Yaran's principle *raison d'être* was to defend the conviction of the Bahá'ís.

But such a defence could only have been possible if the court had respected the law. The lawyers of the Yaran insisted on this outcome, and tried to ensure that the provisions of the Constitution were upheld. In fact, this was why the trial was so protracted and the court sessions indefinitely delayed. The judge wanted to give the impression that he agreed, but also pretended that he had to examine the matter more closely before the prisoners' detention could be changed to bail. As one session after another was postponed because of illegal court proceedings, we lawyers became increasingly concerned that our clients would no longer be very much in favour of our pressing for compliance with the laws. In the end, after three consecutive days of hearings, on 12 June 2010, all these concerns were swept aside and the deadlock was broken by a single sentence from Mahvash Sabet. With great courage and indescribable audacity she stood up on behalf of the Yaran and said, 'Well, the upshot is that you will finally condemn us. We know that and we are ready for death. But we nevertheless believe that the laws must be upheld and that the Bahá'ís in this country should have the right to defend themselves and their faith.'

When Mahvash Sabet and Fariba Kamalabadi were in Ghohardasht, their fellow prisoners had been prohibited from associating with them. However, the behaviour of these two brave women was such that it gradually attracted the respect of the others. Indeed the staunchness of faith and the unfaltering humanity of Mahvash Sabet is worthy of every praise.

Mahnaz Parakand

Note on the Translations

In March 2011 we received, through friends in Iran, a collection of about twenty-five prison poems written by Mahvash Sabet since her arrest in 2008. My mother read them to me and their honesty and compassion moved us both greatly. After I wrote an English version of one of them with her help, she suggested that we work together on the rest. So we embarked on a project of 'translation-by-proxy', my mother and I. She was 83 years old and very frail in health, with little energy to spare. I was handicapped by lack of knowledge, lack of Persian, lack of everything. But since it was the month of Fasting, and we knew the imprisoned Bahá'ís to be fasting too, my mother was determined. Each day of the month of 'Alá that year, which was her last, she substituted poetry for the Fast itself. On learning of this, through friends and family who visited her, Mahvash was so moved that she dedicated a poem to my mother that same April (see p. 115). The procedure we followed was very simple. My mother would first provide a word-for-word draft from the Persian and then, based on her notes, I would try to align the tone of the English translation to the intention of the original. I ended up with a version that depended more on meaning than on music and had less metre than metaphor, but although inevitably approximate, it proved how much the poems merited attention. When we suddenly received a consignment of fifty new originals early that summer, the project assumed serious dimensions. At this point we requested permission from Mahvash herself as well as from her family and the Universal House of Justice to seek a publisher who might be interested in making an English adaptation of these poems accessible to a wider readership.

The new poems seemed more direct, less polished than the first selection. But it was not possible to ask Mahvash about them nor to continue on the translation at that point, because my mother's strength was waning. I had not anticipated that one of the poems (p. 43) would become so personally relevant to us that summer. Nor had I imagined that after her death, my father would offer to complete the task my mother had taken up in the last months of her life. Although he was more accustomed to work on the Bahá'í writings than on poetry, his sense of duty was impeccable, his faithfulness absolute. And so he picked up where she had left off and by the end of 2011, had translated the remaining fifty poems for me to work on, as before.

A free rendition of poems originally written in captivity cannot but lead to approximations. That is why this collection is called an adaptation rather than a true translation. Synonymous phrases and parallel repetitions so dear to Persian convention have been simplified to suit a clearer English style. Familiar metaphors favoured by the Persian ear have been conflated to avoid tautology, and condensed for the sake of sense. The different categories in which these poems have been placed are not of Mahvash's choosing either, but reflect the range of registers she covers even as the title defines the limits in which she has been writing.* However, since the one stipulation she specifically made, when giving permission for this project, was that precise reference to the various prisons in which she has been incarcerated not be included, it was thought to be in keeping with her wishes as well as more helpful to the reader to organize the poems according to subject matter rather than chronology.

Mahvash wrote poetry, by her own admission, as a coping mechanism, as a means of 'perfuming' her daily, mildewed bread (p. 31). Her poems allowed her to speak when words were denied, to talk when no one was listening to her. But unlike many prison poems, hers are not merely a catalogue of hopes and fears, of doubts and desires. Sometimes her verse is a means of historical documentation, a chronicle of what the Bahá'ís have been subjected to since their incarceration: a sort of *Diary*. At other times, she gives us a photo album, in *Portraits*, depicting snapshots of all the other women trapped in prison with her. She writes *Prison Prayers* too, meditations on powerlessness, on loneliness; her poems are plangent with appeal, ardent with hope – for whatever the accusations against her, she is a *Prisoner of Faith*. Mahvash also deploys verse to persuade, to convince, and to motivate herself as well as others to see life in a new light; her training and education are evident in her didactic *Prison Proofs*. But although much of her verse bears witness to her deprivations, she does not dwell on personal suffering. There are rarely any complaints or accusations here, even in the *Dedication*s she offers to members of her family and those she has loved. These poems simply testify to the courage and the despair, the misery and the hopes of thousands of Iranians struggling to survive conditions of extreme oppression.

At the time of writing, Mahvash Sabet is gravely ill in prison, suffering from tuberculosis of the bone. But if her bright spirit still shines though these pages, it is because many mid-wives have attended the

---

* The first selection of poems she sent out of prison was under the eponymous title 'Remember Me'.

birth of her poems at this dark hour. Thanks are first and foremost due to my parents, who made the initial translations. Next I would like to express special gratitude to Professor Farzaneh Milani who helped to hone the early drafts, and to Mahnaz Parakand who wrote the introduction to this volume. I am also indebted to Diane Alai, Mary Victoria, Annabel Knight, and Padideh Sabeti, for their kind support as well as Pippa Tristram and Cathy McCann for their interest in this project. I would also like to express my gratitude to Lorraine Pritchard for her art contribution to the cover, which so exquisitely reflects the many-layered process of reading and writing that has been necessary for the creation of this collection. Above all, I am grateful to May Hofman and Erica Leith for their determination to bring Mahvash to the attention of the world.

Bahiyyih Nakhjavani
France, November 2012

Prison Diary

The Journey of the Seed

I was a worthless seed once, the small kernel of a dream,
which providence had planted near your love's stream.

For a while I sat beside your rippling waters, lingered a while deep in
your soil,
drinking in the crystal waters, trying to understand my own soul.

And after a season of waiting, the husk of my being broke apart
and the open sores of my body, touched by your balm, began to hurt.

I could barely tolerate the pain of being cut off from my past;
I wept bitterly within, groaned,
suffered
saw no future – till at last

I knew what I must do and cast off that old husk of mine
to find this new clothing – of naked, vulnerable skin,

and free from my previous self, I could no more guess then
where I had come from – or where I might be going.

So passing here and there, from talking to listening I grew,
rejoicing in this new freshness, striving towards certitude.

And I saw your beauty shimmering before me in the verdant trees,
and I found you in the gleaming rain drops, stirred by the glad breeze.

And lifting up my arms towards the light of your vast love
I began to dance and grow dappled, reaching for the sun above.

See the blushing branches of my body fluttering beneath these waves,
and my small buds of beauty blossoming, a sea among the leaves!

I'm no longer what I was: an estuary overflows the cistern.
My spring is full of joy now, eager for the fruits of autumn!

But just imagine how many seeds still remain inside –
Hundreds! Ready to burst from my heart with the high tide!

From Evin to Raja'i Shahr

After years in one, we were taken to another prison,
marched to Raja'i Shahr, with weary steps and hard.
Our tearful farewells, like the tight breath of Evin,
lay locked in the heart of this broken-winged bird.

And as our convoy took the unfrequented ways
where we might pass unnoticed and unseen,
we felt the cold winds of revenge blow once again
as they did that cold noon, on the twenty-eighth of Sha'ban.

Through the wide-skirted foothills of proud Elborz
a path's been cut that leads to this narrow cage.
When we approached, the guards drew back the doors,
crimson cheeked on either side, as if ashamed.

Beyond those gates, another world, another race,
a people poisoned and oppressed by woe;
they stared wearily at us, the prisoners we faced,
with sunken eyes, lack-lustre, circled with sorrow.

And as we walked further, step by step, appalled,
as deeper into this penitentiary we crossed,
we heard from behind closed doors, poor girls calling,
crouched behind the shuttered apertures we passed.

At last the last door of the last cage, and we're thrust
in where the exhalation of the dying is our air.
It seemed that all the corpses in the world had cast
their dust over those faces, wan with fear.

There's no space to breathe here, nowhere to sit, to stand
between the earth below, the ceiling overhead.
Sure, God Himself must grieve to see so harsh a hand
ravaging the fruitless branches of these living dead.

The slaughterhouse is always daubed with lovers' blood, it seems,
and so we prayed till dawn, inside that pitch dark cell.
The fire of judgement must have burned so fiercely in Tabriz
that its flames had reached and scorched these very walls.

Each door on every side of all long corridors like this
lead straight towards the same humiliation.
In abattoirs where thought is daily killed like this,
faith is exchanged for hopeless desolation.

Each woman here is penalized for being unaware
that she has wronged the honour of love's rites.
Each one lies prostrate here, and in despair,
for having bartered the sun for the kiss of a sole night.

Each whip is stained with hatred here, as well as blood;
each scourge betrays a woman's shame as well as pain.
And everywhere you look, another sinks to the ground
waiting for Mother Earth to revive her again.

The Curtain

They drew a curtain
tight in front of me.
They twisted a piece of cloth around a rope
and stretched it on a frame before me.
Then they pulled the folds
taut as a wrack on each side of me
– hands hanging loose
and body dangling –
The light was crucified,
the curtain holding it hostage
before my eyes.

Maybe, at some other time than this,
I'll see you face to face
without this screen
between us?

No Boundaries

Eye to eye and knee to knee,
free from what was and what might be,
we peered into our mirrors, dulled with grime,
trying to make out on their sullied surfaces
that shimmering spot where the sun still shines
like gold around the temples of the world's fair bride.
Bewitched by the mountain of love, spell-bound
by the fragrance of green lawns and red geranium.

And all around us and on every side,
echoed disjointed sounds and syllables
– for whatever else they might have been,
these dislocated noises were not words –
while we, like those twin letters, B and E,
were linked together in harmony
eye to eye and knee to knee,
bewitched by the mountain of love, spell-bound
by the fragrance of green lawns and red geranium.

We did not know as we tried to conjure calm,
and still the cacophony with our silences,
we did not know as we tried to reflect the charm
of that bright place in our spotted selves,
how much we could disturb, how much perturb
those extinguished hearts – It's true.
We did not realise what smiles could do.

And so in that hellish misery, we smiled:
at the woman with legs beaten black and blue,
and the insane one with frozen eyes,
and the sick one with her yellow skin,
and the ones who seemed neither men nor women,
and the old ones in the embrace of death,
and the starved ones with shaven heads,
those with scratched cheeks, and others
who had lost their hopes with their teeth,
and the young with yellow, pus-filled wounds
who smelled of rot that would make you shudder,

with voices like rust and thoughts that withered,
and the innocent ones whose looks appealed,
whose fingers clutched, whose voices whined
like clinging tendrils of the anxious columbine.

For in that place of tribulation, a smile was enough
to evoke the fragrance of green lawns, of red geranium;
a single word recalling the sanctity of humankind
gathered together the broken hearts and made them whole.
And so before too long the women began to look
first secretly, then openly, inside the pages of the book.

And one sweet girl
– learning to read for the first time –
when she saw how separate syllables
joined together to make meaning –
oh! how her eyes shone with the beauty of it!
how her laughter rang with beauty of it!
How beautifully she spelled out what she had seen.

We did not understand that others,
Ignorant of how letters linked together,
would want to separate one from another.
We could not guess that these illiterate ones,
given to subtraction rather than addition,
would go so far, not only to shun
but to try and erase us from the lexicon.

But by then most had understood;
most had heard the harmony and realized
that different syllables unite to make a word.
And some had even begun to turn the pages
of the open book, had begun to read
that there were no boundaries
between what's seen and said,
linked together in unity
eye to eye and knee to knee.

Remembering the Sea

I shut my eyes in this weary cell
where the circle of friendship is shattered
and the pattern of thought broken.
I shut my eyes, for the path is dreary
across this ceiling and along these walls.
Every exit barred and bolted,
and all acts tedious, repetitious,
where the circle of friendship is shattered
and the pattern of thought broken.

Outside the sky was blue, so clear
with the wind and the waves, so beautiful!
What a sea of joy it was! How near –
with the surging waters and the boat
and lovers swimming everywhere
and a peace that was free from fear.

*(He said, I shall eventually defeat you, whoever you are, wherever you
may be.)*

But I cannot forget how soft the sand,
how many the children playing beside the sea.
Passion and joy – the game and the ball!
How gleefully they built their castles studded with shells,
brimming with happiness, playing without shame.

(How unjust the judge was, how cruel the bitter judgement.)

Attar of rose can drift on the empty air;
the purest water can rise from the blackest earth.
Spring spills over and is ready to flow, like the sea.

*(When the final verdict was delivered,
he estimated our lives as completely worthless, saying,
Go wait for your freedom for the next twenty years.)*

O youth, where have you gone? And what become?
It's time to pack your bags, make ready for reunion.

God's speed and the fair winds of chance be yours!
Brim over then, go sway and flow with the sea.
Home is lovely, beautiful; it longs for your return.

(And when will we experience that sweet pain,
that giddy sensation of returning?
And what home might we come to then? And where?
O woe! for my bird has flown its nest, and I have none.
All my passion for a home is lost and gone.
So what's the point in being free again?)

The Friends

No hand reaches to protect this hundred-petalled rose,
no door opens at our knock; the bell's out of reach.
We're fallen and abased on love's long road
without wine at the banquet nor a cup to quench.
No ray from the Unseen is here to lift our gloom;
nights are pitch, air stagnant, and moon pale.
Not a single messenger brings comfort to this room;
not a star nor any orb lights up this dismal cell.
No sign of justice here, no hope of it anymore;
impossible to touch the judge's robe or beg mercy at his feet.
Bleak vision, fearful future, a world busy at its wars,
so what prospect is there to escape this weary fate?
To the desert walker, all seas are fading mirages.
To one dead of thirst, the spring of certitude has dried.
We shout as loudly as we can but our voices too are caged,
and day after day death is denied, as well as aid.
No one listens, no one hears this wingless bird.

Prison Walls

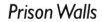

Cocoon

There's a part of me that keeps mourning
for the soft cocoon where I lay,
a part of me that keeps pining
for the delicate chrysalis smashed and destroyed
before my eyes that day.

I'm tossed to and fro, from here to there,
caught between compulsions;
I'm thrown left and right and back and forth,
longing for the freedom of flight and yet
craving those soft consolations.

When my soul broke free, a part of me
thrilled at the lift of its arc,
but another shrank back in cowering fear
from the threatening fires, from the lowering smoke
that awaited me in here.

All this makes me wonder greatly
about contrary desires.
There's something in me approves of flying,
applauds the thought of bravely dying,
yet I weep for the cocoon's demise.

The Sparrow

One day, returning from the prison walk
I met a sparrow taking the air too, on my way.
It was pecking at a piece of frozen bread,
a cold crumb lying between us in the snow.
'You and I are both hungry prisoners,' I said.
At that, it instantly let go the crumb and flew away,
and I thought, 'Are you less than this sparrow?
Why don't you drop the bread too, like this bird?
Why can't you free yourself from crumbs – and words?'

And This Is Where I Stand Sometimes

And this is where I stand sometimes
looking up at the sky
staring through that narrow gap
between two sheets of rusted steel
cutting me off from the heavy sky.

It's always overcast, this ceiling,
this lid that lies over my life,
this piece of cloth that hangs
like the greasy hem of a dirty skirt
over this alienated city.
But I see swallows, on occasion,
breathless, flitting, and uncertain,
darting here and twisting there in greeting.
Are they saying 'good morning' to me?
A cat comes too, from time to time, and laughs,
offering complimentary salutations
in sly tones of high deception.
I've seen two or three honey bees as well
circling round the stem of a fake flower,
drinking grief-juice, sucking sorrow.
And I'm so stirred by these sights that afterwards
I lie sleepless, imagining the sound of breathing,
asking myself, 'Is that the wind that's rustling?'
Asking, 'What is it saying? What is happening?
Is someone speaking, telling me something?'
Once, in the heart of winter,
a woman called out to me in greeting, 'Happy Feast!'
And another, hearing her, cried out with joy,
'Is it the time then? Has Naw-Rúz arrived at last?'

But instead of blades of fresh wheat sprouting
there were only thorns and thistles growing,
and sudden snakes writhing over the ground,
and a stag standing at the walls of each town
with the heart of a maid caught between its horns,
and a woman, veiled in doubt, who was trembling
as the night rose pitch and black outside –

and I saw it all through one of the narrowest cracks
in the world: this window where I stood, waiting.

Where are you, tell me, for I can't see too far.
I can only hear the breathing of the flowers from here.
I can only eavesdrop from behind this senseless window
on the throbbing of hearts. I can only hear
the terrible sound of delicate lady-birds
being whipped and crushed and beaten.

It's not you I hear.
Where are you, tell me?
For I can't see too far.

My City

I want a house high on Elborz,
where I can look from the summit down;
for I can't bear to keep living here
in this suffocating underground.
And between its pleated skirts and foothills,
sweet jasmine and nasturtium I will grow,
and fill my house with lilies and narcissus
to shade this fevered place below.

This is a city of the sleeping, parched and sick,
a city of the sacrificed who'd sell all for a smoke.
Hearts are estranged here, cruel beneath these clouds:
this is a city with a grim look, where none smiles aloud.
It's a home for separated selves without occupation,
where friends exile one another, and know of no relations,
a metropolis of the ignorant, a capital for the despised,
a ruin of lost creatures addicted to telling lies,
of women given up to shame, accustomed to abuse,
sad and embittered souls, afflicted by misuse.

In the dead heart of this city we've forgotten how to speak.
Sense has been stolen from our sentences; we can only shriek.
Coherence has been lost here, nothing intelligible is heard;
kindness grows inarticulate, eroded the gentle words.
Only the walls of separation still tower high above –
and a dull round of daily routine numbs the groove.

How I long to learn a different language,
use syntax with another tense,
command a new vocabulary
to express a brighter glance.
How I yearn to find unspoken words
that all instantly understand,
a sense beyond the sentence heard,
the greater dance –

I can't stay any longer in this suffocating place.
Come with me! Pitch your tent on Elborz high above!
Speak with a different voice, show me another face;
don't linger here, come climb the peaks of love!

Lights Out

Weary but wakeful, feverish but still
fixed on the evasive bulb that winks on the wall,
thinking surely it's time for lights out,
longing for darkness, for the total black-out.

Trapped in distress, caught in this bad dream,
the dust under my feet untouchable as shame,
flat on the cold ground, a span for a bed,
lying side by side, with a blanket on my head.

And the female guards shift, keeping vigil till dawn,
eyes moving everywhere, watching everyone,
sounds of the rosary, the round of muttered words,
fish lips moving, the glance of a preying bird.

Till another hour passes in friendly chat,
in soft talk of secrets or a sudden spat,
with some snoring, others wheezing
some whispering, rustling, sneezing –
filling the space with coughs and groans,
suffocated sobs, incessant moans –

You can't see the sorrow after lights out.
I long for the dark, the total black-out.

Bear This in Mind

When you pass by
a heap of rotting rats
bear this in mind:
they might not all be dead.
They might just be lying there,
lying and pretending.
Because no one bothers
the dead round here.

Loneliness

I said: 'Give me a definition of loneliness.'
You said: 'When no one's there beside you.'
I said: 'What if you're even lonelier than that?'
You said: 'Then when there's no one to love you.'
I said: 'Define the greatest loneliest of all.'
You said: 'When no one understands you.'

The Great Outdoors

When you finally leave this sultry atmosphere
and arrive at last in some green pasture far outdoors –

Go lose yourself under an endless waterfall,
and sit beneath the teeming and relentless rain.
Go warm yourself under the benediction of the sun
and speak with no one but the flowers of the meadow.
Let your heart brim with the lovely and the beautiful,
fill up your arteries with the rapture of the joyful,
and let love sing to your very nerve endings
till all your senses synchronize once more
with this pure scent, this peaceful fragrance
of the great outdoors.

In fact, it is quite enough for me
just to look forward to that vast immensity
                                        – of air –
even if I never reach it, never get there.

Someone Must

Someone must want this life,
someone must understand this life,
someone must try to explain what the meaning is
of living a life as meaningless as this.
Someone must justify this unending dark,
must speak about the hope and heartache
of this perplexed, this lost and bewildered people.
Someone must want more to life than this,
must surely understand that this is not all life is.

Revenge

What a clamour! What a rage! What roars of wrath!
I want to go to bed to escape this thunder.
What furious anger spewing out of the heart!
What blood caught between fire and cinder.

A brawl has been raised by a bitter being,
a wretch rich only in her own regrets,
a soul made vicious by life's void,
a prisoner of her very ignorance.
But what hidden ironies still lie ahead,
what reprisals await her on this road – ?
How many the wayfarers, self-chained,
are heirs of injustice, yoked to its load!

Why make demands of these shattered souls
who wander round here pathless, lost?
What's to be got from these heart-sick girls?
Can a tempest reap harvests from such ghosts?
Like a dragon ready to waylay the unwary
you inspect these throngs of broken ones,
then with a nod, a nudge, an intimation,
you begin the assault and do your worst.
Slander lurks here in every corner;
each trap has been laid for another's fall,
but when violence begins and the howls arise,
woe to her whose name's yelled loudest,
the one against whom all hands are raised!

The ringleader, safe from harm's way,
lets loose the flood, provokes the savage tide.
She goads her followers on, adds fuel to fire,
and as the fight erupts, observes it, satisfied.
Some hurl themselves with wild abandon in the fray;
others try to avoid it, and a frightened few
hide in the corners, shivering at the show.
But when the ancient rage subsides at last,
then cries and groans and sighs lift up on every side.
Then anger ebbs and weary tears begin to fall

with the blood that's spilled so recklessly around.
For thousands of new regrets have been conceived
and a hundred fresh hurts have left ugly stains;
hearts are now bruised far deeper than the wounds
and seeds of vengeance are starting to sprout again . . .

Each time a wave of mutiny is raised
our feet sink deeper in its mire and mud
and no one ever comes to give us aid
in this heart of pain, this hurricane of blood.

The shriek of the birds at dawn confirms
that it's long since nightingales sang in this garden.
But though we say nothing, our silence affirms
that we weep for the violets hidden among these thorns.

I have written a message on a nasturtium leaf
and hung it on my door, like a charm.
It says: 'There's a warm heart waiting here,
and a mother's open arms.'

I Rose Up Again

Sunk in myself
one hot, dusty morning,
walking alone in the prison yard
I wandered along the length of the wall,
pondering the meaning of isolation and of doors,
brooding on all these endless barriers and bolts and bars
and all the pointless fights and skirmishes and wars,
and considering where I was and why the abuse
was being flung against me, I began to wonder
whether these confines really defined
the limits of my self.

And then I saw
in the heart of the tar
in the middle of the road
from the dry earth's blistered core
and the stones in the lumbering tarmac
deep down from within a crack
in the ground at my feet
a few leaves sprouting,
green and neat.

And some days later
there they were again! Bright green!
Now, in every nook and cranny, all around
as far as the eye could see, there were thistles growing,
thousands of leaves and stems and offshoots
scattered far and wide and bursting out
of the prison yard!

And I said to myself,
'Are you less than a weed then?
Where's the life in your roots gone?
Where's growth in your leaves, your stem?
No stirring in you at all? For shame!'
And at that I felt a surge of the sap
of spirit blaze within.

I'd become weak and weary and had fallen down,
but the thistle made me rise again.
Back on my feet I stand firm and green growing,
filled the power of thought again.

Prison Portraits

The Perfume of Poetry

Alone, under the bare branches
of the pomegranate tree,
I feel the weight of these captive women
lie heavily on me.

A group of them murmur in a corner
beneath a broken wall,
while younger ones, distracted, flutter
to and fro and wail.

One of the captives perches a while
here under my poor shade,
her fluting notes rise only to fall again
disconsolate and sad.

Others stoop over their laundry,
do their washing in rows,
bending beneath the line already bowed
under the weight of clothes.

Autumn has crept upon us unawares
and stripped our fruitless boughs,
but the spring of your kind hand still
strokes our wintry brows.

One old woman can barely stand, but you
still rise in her defence,
singing out how wronged she is, how lonely,
bowed by innocence.

But all I do is drown in the drained drops
from the veins of a girl.
All I can do is dissolve at the losses of one
too young to be so pale.

And when a woman is forced to stamp
the warrant with her thumb,

I forget my own shames, choke at hers –
humiliated, heart-wrung.

And if another escapes execution somehow,
the chance of a rare reprieve,
my heart leaps up at her happiness, thrills
at her cries of relief.

And if a weary addict moans without ceasing,
moans and cries through the night,
I despair with her, grow ever more anguished
till the break of light.

And that is why I need a balm to perfume
this camphor-tasting bread,
a light to cast on these yellowed faces,
a breath to lift these heads.

That's why I send my waves and ripples
across this stagnant pond,
its surface seething, its depths torpid
with anger, all trust gone –

I write if only to stir faint memories of flight
in these wing-bound birds,
to open the cage of the heart for a moment
trapped without words.

For how can one not faint for these women,
beaten so brutally?
How can one not fear for them, suffering
such tyrannical cruelty?

Alone, under the bare branches
of the pomegranate tree,
I feel the weight of these captive women
lie heavily on me.

Billows of Smoke

My lungs reek with your smoke
and as the grey clouds rise and swell
I glance over your shoulder and see
how bleak the world looks from your cell.

You've taken refuge in melancholy tales
to escape worse dreams;
you've reached the farthest frontiers here
but still deny your shames.
Your broken-hearted cries rend heaven
from this hell without respite,
but your stony stare stays fixed the while
on the hands of those you meet.
You would sell the clothes from off your back
for a puff of a single Zar,
but since the world's transformed to smoke,
time means nothing any more.
From the restless tides of your erratic rage
clouds of impatience rise.
You feel so betrayed, so tricked and cheated
that you rail against the skies.
Oh howling one, veiled in billows of smoke,
what are these floods of woe?
Life's brief flame is housed in glass:
once broken, blood will flow.
Alas, sweet girl, for your lonely griefs,
for the wrongs that have crippled your thoughts:
you lie curled up there like a yellow leaf
which has lost touch with its roots.

Since there's no surer road to ruin
than walking in these ways
I prefer to take the quicker route
than talking in this haze.

So here's something small to bring
a little colour to your cheek:
a poem, full of love that's fresh
as a poppy, and just as weak.

Lonely Prisoner

Your home was uprooted and swept away
in the flood that roared through this land,
your body was whipped and battered
by a husband's cruel hand;
your eyes have grown sleepless,
your pain lies concealed,
you've given up all hope of cure
of being healed.
After living in anguish,
year after silent year,
you've utterly despaired
of ever leaving here,
nothing remains to you now
but that single, precious frame,
that photograph which you press
to your heart and kiss, again and again,
lifting your eyes towards the entrance way,
unable to escape these futile, heart-sick days.

The husband who oppressed you is content;
your marriage is in ashes, you the only mourner.
Your children have become estranged and sadly absent,
leaving you lost, abandoned, and forgotten in this corner.
Your cup of sorrow has been filled with bitterness to the brim,
and life's no more to you than an empty bubble on its surface;
it seems that once you tumbled headlong in this dustbowl,
there was no one who gave a damn for your disgrace.
Parched as a cut flower lying in these stagnant waters,
you wait to hear the fatal verdict, know your doom;
despite your prayers for mercy, pleas for reprieve,
the days stretch out before you, empty and alone.
Remorse runs rampant in your deserts of regret
as you brood over the prison tasks you do;
how you resent life's wasted harvests now!
How shrunk the pittance that's your due!

You've barely enough clothes to wear, or a warm dress,
leave alone the will to notice me.
What can I do, what dare I offer you –
a poor captive who can never make you free?

What recourse is there, after all, but to shed tears for you,
gathering them like pearls here, in my skirt for you?

The Sacrifice

You are always seated there, whenever I pass by,
a prisoner of grief, to misery fast bound,
as if there were no secret wisdoms to be learned
from our time here, and its uncertain end.
Your cup of self is drained of knowing wine,
depleted of desire, sapped of illusions;
like the varying wind that veers from dusk till dawn,
you are the helpless child of your emotions.
One moment, laughter ripples from your heights;
the next, your stream plunges deep down and dives
beneath the dry and barren rocks, without a trace,
without a hope of ever reaching the sea waves.
You cast about this wasteland, blowing here and there,
like a seed thirsting in the wilderness,
with neither fear of the approaching storm, nor faith
to expect more than a drop of rain, at best.
Each passing whirlwind seizes you in his embrace
and throws you on the dust before you realize;
if you only knew how quickly he would turn aside,
how callously he would treat your trust, how full of lies.

If I hold you to my heart, it is a silent prayer
that you might rise above this cage and truly fly.
The finest diamonds in the world are meagre stones
compared with the gem you lightly toss away.
If I rub your feet, it is to conceal my tears
for the treasures ransacked from God's store;
if only I could show you the light you have within,
for you're unique: what would you more?
Your eyes are heirs of the sun's brightest beams;
it rises in your cheeks and sets there too.
Your lips smile petals that flower when you laugh;
even the nightingales steal songs from you.
My heart aches, for you do not seem to know
the worth of that subtle inner star.
If only you could see the lovely prisoner who lies
prostrate in who you think you are.
How did you come to inherit this unhappy fate?

For whom do you sacrifice your very worth?
Why have you let misfortune ruin your life,
to wander so bereft along this path?

O, let the fragile shoots grow green again
and their hope rise within your soil!
Let these seeds take root and don't condemn
the jewels entrusted to your soul.

Turmoil

I live in the middle of endless turmoil,
sleep in tumult, wake in turmoil,
ride my broken thoughts through tumult,
surrounded by the sounds of turmoil.
I keep still in this confounded din
but I cannot quieten the cacophony;
even confinement's cup of solitude
is cruelly noise-filled to the very lip.
So trapped in darkness I step into sunlight,
choked by tumult, I choose to breathe jasmine;
though born of water, I can only burn
with compassion for these suffering women.

God is as simple as an apple for them,
a reminder of that far-off garden.
God is a fresh loaf of bread for them,
recalling the festal board, the happy table.
God is the mere thought of freedom to them
in this pit of bottomless depression;
God Is the echo of the sacred in them,
quiet amid this clamorous lamentation.

No woman here stays hungry for too long:
fed on miseries, nourished by despair.
No woman suffers hurt or injury alone:
deceiving herself, betrayed by others.
All women talk of loneliness in here:
mourning old friends, bewailing lovers.
And yet once free, what refuge have they left?
What shelter, and what home elsewhere?

See that silent woman seated in the corner,
mourning a love that has forsaken her to this?
She's thinking of the baby cradled in her womb
who must inherit poverty and distress.
If you reach a hand out to caress a head here,
a hundred stars shine in the eyes;

if you utter a single word of love here,
it is like water quenching furious fires.

After a while, I see what folly it is
to search for human dignity in vain:
If I'm in this prison now, it's only because
I've committed the crime of love again.

The Captive

Her hair is tossed by the hand of the wind,
her smile is as pale as glass;
her cheeks are so bright and brittle
they break bitterly as she laughs.
Whenever she talks of the bygone days,
her eyes bleed stories;
from the day her world blew apart in the storm
she lost all vital forces.
She gave up her children to fate
because of their father's hostility,
and motherhood withered inside her heart
with love's mortality.
She's been galled by imprisonment ever since,
one more of the nameless;
the wounds are old, but the pain is fresh,
without remedy, and hopeless.
For fifteen years the gallows' spectre
has hung over her head;
and all she can feel is the rope round her neck
and the terror of being dead.
Her eyes half-closed, she's asleep where she sits,
more dead than trying to wake,
but as soon as the chair jerks from under her feet
she starts up in stark shock.
The world has shrivelled and meaning has shrunk
as colourless as her clothes;
the war and peace of her friendships depend
on childish sorrows and joys.
She is sick of this anguish, she's ill with distress,
she's trapped in torment,
like moss that clings to a stone in a pond,
she drowns within her depths.
She speaks of remorse and wails with regret
but has no faith in forgiveness;
though when she falls silent it proves she believes
most ardently in darkness.

As I gaze in those eyes that are fixed on mine
I see only a burned out star,
like a beacon that flickers far off on a hill
in the night's unending core.

How long will it burn? How long can she last
before giving up in this prison?
How long can I sit here, how long will I watch
this mother crouched on a coffin?

Times Gone By

Brief dust mote drifting in a beam of light,
lost in the diurnal round of day and night,
mourning in midnight's lap, asleep at noon,
your sun changing places with the moon.
Forever hankering over times gone by;
forever dreaming of lost opportunities.
Hoping for fancied seas, illusory skies,
Farhad, Shirin and their eternal love stories –

You're loaded with the burden of remorse:
a heavy weight, a futile encumbrance.
You think it's change that you anticipate,
but it's evident for what, for whom you wait.
You still desire a man's desire for you;
though tired of guilt, you still assume his guilt.
Though he denies you recompense, you deny
that he broke the salt cellar and stole the salt.

How much longer will you wait for love's return?
How many nights before you rise to meet the dawn?
When will you cast these veils and fantasies aside,
this brooding over times and fairy tales gone by?
I see you freezing in the midst of burning coals,
weeping whole oceans with your glittering tears,
cast down by foes, abandoned in infernal wells,
oblivious that the caravan has come, has gone.

Come, spread your wings, soar up to higher realms,
beyond the moon that mocks, the dreams that fly.
Or else look down at the traces of this passing caravan
and see what a mote of dust you are upon the way.

But you do neither, brooding only of the times gone by,
Losing days and nights in search of lost nights and days.

When She Died

A woman died here, early this morning.

When she died
the waves of her breath beating,
one by one, against these clammy sands,
failed at last to pull back all the wet shells piled inside
and shattered one by one like glass against the shore.

When she died,
the light in her face fading,
yellow as the blown grass of the wilderness,
dimmed at last, her glance no longer fixed as she gave up
the task of breathing: one long sigh and then no more.

And when she died,
a female guard uncaring,
came at last to stuff her in a bag, indifferent,
as if she were no more than a branch of pine needles dried up.
It was as simple as that, the morning that she died.

No one asked why the moth's wings had turned blue;
No one wondered what she had been thinking
or whether the chrysanthemum had murmured to her,
bending at her ear beside death's door.
And no one asked who'd lit the candle at her coming
or if her going had been what she'd dreamed before.

All they said was – well,
the poor thing is free at last –
And I witnessed it.

Her bundle of things, so frail,
an ant could have carried it off like a grain of wheat –
And I witnessed it.

Her food a crumb of bread, so small,
that a worm in the water could have swallowed it –
And I witnessed it.

But behind her glassy eyes there lay a faint bloom of tranquillity,
and her mouth was filled with the *ghazals* of humility.
Her lips were lined with the clear azure of the skies
and her cheeks were pale as the moon playing with sunrise –
And I witnessed it.

Maybe someone was coming to meet her from afar
to greet her with a branch of blossoming light,
for the tips of her fingers had become translucent.

Or maybe someone was taking her by the hand
and was leading her perhaps to other lands,
who knows? Maybe she found a home at last,
just big enough for the sense of a prayer.

Or perhaps someone took her to see God
up in the higher realms somewhere.
And maybe He gave her a shelter there,
a threshold she might call her own,
and offered her just enough shade for joy,
for a mouthful of peace, for the taste of love.

And maybe God, at least, believed in her sufferings.

The Land of Nightingales

I come to you, with an ardent heart,
from a country of dusty birds,
from a land where the nightingale is hoarse,
and song-birds have grown dull and coarse,
and girls are prostitutes without choice,
and even babies have drugged voices:
this is where I live now.

Once, as the senile crows were praying
among these throat-locked birds,
I heard my name being called from far,
and when I turned to run back here
a woman approached like a siren's wail,
her face as white as the plastered wall:
this is where I live now.

I come from an unprotected region
where the swallows are thin and poor;
from a country cursed by contrary winds
where even the youngest are paper thin
and tossed in the streets from door to door
blown about without even a guarantor:
this is where I live now.

Someone mocked me for sitting once
by a woman at the stoning well:
a girl whose cup filled with scarlet breath
yet who still smiled, still laughed at death,
and that other who dressed up so fine each night
before hiding in a black bag out of sight:
this is where I live now.

I don't fear the taste of this bitter life
but a flower has soured in my heart;
it has made me inured to the taste of gall.
See that woman drawing near, so thin and pale?
Tell her that I'm worried about her breath,

for it lacks the composure borne of faith
in this place where I live now.

There are no roses here, no nightingales left anymore:
It's a land where even the swallows have grown thin and poor,
where the bird of the heart is unprotected, without any guarantor.

Sonya

Twenty-seven year old Sonya
beautiful face but tired and weary,
she eyes me distantly, her black eyes cold,
pulling away, confused and wary,
as though she were feeling scared, unsafe,
with a luminous complexion dulled by grief.
Sonya dear, talk about yourself.

'I was a spoilt child
surrounded by vanities, by blessings,
raised by a single mother
for whom I was all things.'

She sits alone now, in her pain,
a few premature white strands
streaking her black elfin tresses.
Sonya dear, tell me about yourself.

'I was fourteen, on my way to school
when a Mercedes Benz, the latest model,
stopped alongside me. That was the end
although I thought it was the beginning
for my marriage was inspired by love at first.
But it came to no good at the last.
My husband was a criminal who broke the laws.
We led high-class lives, seemed rich people,
had endless material goods, money unaccountable.
But fear always prevailed, from neighbours and police,
until all that I had left was a single suitcase.
I grew weary of his tawdry friendships,
of spending months on end in filthy hotels,
of always being frightened, on the run.
In the end I ran out of patience at playing wife
and refused to go on with that life.
My "No!" rent the marriage veil,
and led to divorce by mutual consent.'

Her eyelids are swollen, her eyebrows thin,
Her lips once beautiful are lumpy, oddly blue;
there are dark stains mottling her teeth too.
Sonya dear, please tell me more.

'After some time I was free, free at last.
My mother was living with me then
but I still craved a different love, feeling
outgrown, alienated and alone.
One day a man approached me on the street,
and whispered 'Crack? Alcohol? What are you for?
I have everything you need, all kinds – and know
a place where you can get more.'
I liked him, let him take me there and then
to some dead-end place, a drug haven.
A single puff, just one escapade from home,
I thought, and that was it.
I was on my way.
From crack to the bottle
and from high to low.
Day and night I was either on the hunt
for drugs or using them, either completely out
or in a total daze from hour to hour.
After some time my poor mother discovered it.
She found me dazed and understood.
How frightened she was and confused –
but she was determined that I should give it up.
She did everything to help me break the habit.
Her head would droop, her tears would flow;
and I would throw myself at her feet
hearing her silent prayers and whispers.
And I did give it up, for a while.
But a repentant wolf will always end up getting killed.
I stopped and started up again;
I dropped and picked it up again.
The wheel turned round and round
as I tried and failed to escape these bonds.'

Sonya, did it make you happy?
She lifts her head and looks straight at me

and my question, penetratingly,
eyes deep-sunken, skin wax-pale, bruised blue
exuding a strong odour of tobacco.

'Addiction offers no pleasure,
it gives no joy, no inward peace.
Addiction is a sickness with one cure:
searching for drugs from door to door.
Addiction means always needing more
knowing that even this brings no relief
offers nothing but a brief escape,
a foul nightmare between two voids,
even when you think you've run away,
you're back to where you were before.
Escaping from yourself is hardly worth
the price of that return. And what a price!'

So where does all the money come from, Sonya?

'There's no alternative.
You have to pay.
Your need for the stuff increases every day.
And once you're high
you'll do anything to stay that way
including being a pusher too,
doing everything that degrades you:
theft, prostitution
sleeping in the streets
and finally prison.
You try to keep going for a while
but you soon find
that you can't stand, can't walk
can't move anymore, leave alone talk.
You're totally addicted
either by injection, inhalation
or whatever else you may have heard.'

After that who could say another word?

Prison Prayers

Remember Me

Whenever you're feeling captive, like a bird,
whenever you're cornered, like a weary stranger,
whenever you're lost, and see no way ahead,
thinking of home with joy but with no way there –
remember me.

Whenever your cup of wine is drained of love,
whenever your spring's deprived of the flower's scent,
whenever your cheeks are wet with lonely grief
as you run through valleys of bewilderment –
remember me.

Whenever a friend plays music to relieve your heart,
plucking unhappiness away with plaintive hope;
whenever your sorrow eases as you lift your hands
and supplicate for that barred door to open –
remember me.

Whenever the morning breeze brings messages of love
and hopes to you of sweet reunion;
whenever dear ones soothe your burning heart –
remember me, as I mourn here alone.

O servant of that mighty manifestation,
witness of that One adorned with heavenly grace;
O listener of His command, and essence of compassion
who treads the dust before that king's beloved face!
Remember me, for I am naught without you,
a columbine with none to cling to but you,
a beggar at your feet, dependent on you,
whose very life relies entirely on you.
You are the spirit and I, the body only:
and yet we are united and intact, a single rhyme.
You are the essence of the word, I its frail symbol –
mesmerized by your beauty, in love with your sweet name.
See me, detached, rejoicing in this talisman;
remember me, thrilled at the very thought of you.
Come to me, mindful, whatever my condition;

give me the signal and I'll give up my life for you.
How lightly in your hands lie the reins of my breath,
how sweetly your melodies assuage my moans;
how many love songs have you written to appease my grief,
how much you have sustained this suffering one!

So bring me some glad tidings from afar now –
for my eyes are fixed forever on that door!

If It Were Your Will

If it were your will
the sun would rise
from where it never rose before.

If it were your will
the rain would fall
on this parched and deserted shore.

If it were your will
a breeze would freshly blow
across this wilderness, make it a meadow.

If it were your will
these timorous birds
would chirp inside their cages, like *bulbuls* in song.

If it were your will
flowers would bloom
from the breath of these wronged ones.

But alas, alas –
if it is not your will
what use is there
in this poor prayer
of a withered seed beneath dead soil?

Oh woe, for if it is not your will,
your will, O omnipotent One,
what use is there
in this poor prayer
of a withered seed beneath dead soil?

At Such a Time You'll Come

I fear that time
when patience will no more be mine
when brittle hope will have been blown away,
its kindness all have gone,
when the wind will have scattered me
and my eyes will have strayed from the path – O!
if no door opens to me then, not one –
I will know for sure it is that time
when you will come again.

The Sun

I depend on my own shadow,
owe my perseverance to the sun:
O sun of mine! Where are you? Please shine on!

From these layered afflictions,
there's no refuge from the dark but one.
O sun of mine! Where are you? Please shine on!

Cloudy Days

Though I'm sick and tired of the dull round of clouds,
I'll not beg you for sunny skies,
O compelling one!

I know all too well of what worth are the sighs
and pious exhalations of a weed
growing in this jungle.

And I've also learned at last that whatever you decide
shall invariably come to pass,
O compelling one.

So I must try to read what lies beneath these clouds
and wait patiently for the beams
of the inevitable sun.

See how I've finally turned out to be the sort of woman
you wanted me to become –
O compelling one?

The Loneliness of the Stranger

With our backs to the future, our faces to the past,
the years go by and we're all still here:
strangers in our loneliness.

With my back to the future, my face to the past,
holed up in a corner without access to light
I'm still here: a stranger in my loneliness.

Ploughing the soil of the heart
watering the seeds of thought
colouring the tulips of the mind,
busily watching the feelings shift, the seasons change:
but always and forever a stranger in my loneliness.

And as she drinks the stagnant water
of this upside-down life,
As she chokes on the stagnant water
of this inside-out place,
in this back-to-front world,
the stranger keeps longing in her loneliness,
longing for her prayers to be answered.

Dust

I drew near the mirror
to see myself better.
It said, 'Go and get lost!
You're nothing but dust.'

The Earth

We think we know about its laws, its gravity:
we think we understand
the way the little seed falls on damp soil,
the way the soil feels ready to reveal its secret soul,
the way the earth is generous in anticipating roots,
the tender way it loves those first frail shoots.
But we don't realize how crude, how ignorant and base
our footsteps on it are, sometimes.

How dare we strut about, unworthy as we are
and tramp these green fields with so little grace!
How abject, faced by the frank, open plains
and chaste generosity of this noble place!
Who else would give us gifts so deep, so wide –
show more humility towards us, manifest less pride?

Drag me down to the water's depths
– so arrogant and cold!
Pull me down from the floating tide
and drown this wretched weed.
Be rid of me, for love, be done –
for compared to this nobility, I've none
and weighed against earth's worth,
I don't deserve a single breath.

Beaming Up

Since you look small to me, and far,
it's surely because you are so high.
You seem more distant than a star
twinkling brightly in night's sky.

I suppose that is because you live
at the domed zenith of high heaven.
Can you even see this dirty sieve,
this pit of hell where I've been driven?

Aim for my shining eyes, beloved,
– two tiny stars that beam in this dark night –
I've turned them to the skies, beloved,
to seek out and reflect your light.

The Star

My heart aches for the silence of that star,
parched with thirst as the dry ground for the brackish rain,
fervently in love with the falling waters.

My heart longs for the soft breath of the wind,
blowing over the lonely pool where the reflected moon
trembles below the lawn in the blue waters.

Dull wits can never know the speed of light,
or why the clipped tresses of the sleeping willow dip so
precisely on the green shoulders of the waters.

In what part of that enticing crimson rose
does the wilful attar bloom? Where's joy exactly hidden
in this garden, glinting like the gilt of secret waters?

And why do we pass the days of our brief lives
so painfully, so sadly? Why so solemn and so sere?
Won't that bright star cast joy at last on this night's waters?

Limits

I've come to the end; not much is left.

The blood in my narrow veins is like an old postman
creaking up a dark and ruinous path on a decrepit bicycle.
My lungs are filled with the poison of this air,
rank and stagnant with the taste of camphor and of soot.
My ears are deafened by the shrieks around me
in this stinking, fetid, dead-end place.
I am hemmed in by thoughts so limited, so closed,
that I can barely distinguish my own pain
from the intransigent perversity of those
whose idea of unity consists
in shattering relationships;
whose notion of knowledge is built
on what they do not want to know and never ask;
whose definition of belief depends
on all they do not seek and therefore cannot find,
on all they do not hear and therefore cannot understand.
The corruption of those who cannot think and yet give orders
drains me of my capacities, defines my limitations.

Oh! Who is it that holds me back from your embrace?
I can no longer hear the beating of your heart.
Where is the memory of your perfumed breath, your face?
I have forgotten the warm sound of your voice.

See how little is left of my spiritual capacities.

Indifference

At this time, when I burn patiently in these fires,
when my limbs blaze, and my flames bloom like lilies,
flickering high as a beacon shining from the hill tops,
even as I lie blistered and scorched down here,
at this time when I see my way clear,
see the blood-red path before me hot and searing,
let me step onward and keep walking,
let me never falter, never fear –

But woe, if ever the flame were once to wane
to waver and to fade from all this pain.
Woe, if I were to turn ash cold again
and if the dust of indifference were to stain
my spirits, freeze me in my chains –

For who, alas, would then be grieved,
or remember the meaning of my life,
or the worth of what I once believed?

Prison Proofs

Illusory Distinctions

Such frontiers, borders, boundaries of illusion!
Such barriers of fancy, distinctions of delusion!
These confines of time, these limits of space
create unreal riddles, fences without sense.

Zero point is where I stand to be at one with you:
where infinity chimes with eternity and still is true.
Zero point is beyond either time or place:
if the earth turns on a single axis, it has no face.
So why create distinctions between day and night
when even pines grow quietly in the moonlight?
In this prison they insist on temporal crimes
saying this is such and such a day, month, year, and time.
But what difference does it make in the world's giddy stage,
on which convoluted hook they choose to hang your cage?
And what's the point of making sense by inventing halves
in the narrow language of identity, the shrunk prose of selves?

Blame creates boundaries between us, don't you see?
It's an old game played by sun and moon and earth – of rivalry;
a taut game of power which has chequered all our lives,
an endless game repeating revolutions round the skies.
But I don't want to take part in power games any more.
I prefer to raise a white flag, pure as any flower,
a simple banner of resistance bearing the word: 'Love',
a word whose myriad meanings have spawned endless proofs.
In fact since there's no common understanding of this word
it is the final barrier we must remove!

And so my longing to explain it to you aright
flows through me like pure water, binding root to earth,
rises in me like sap journeying towards the light,
shines in me as warm as the core of a sun beam,
breathes in me like a leaf's veins growing green,
or a vase holding a budding branch up to be seen,
or a branch bending over the neighbour's high wall,
full of new blossoms, laden with soft scent for all.

My love is a single rose that offers you this plea:
what good can illusory distinctions do for you and me?

Floodgates

Let the well-spring of my songs and poems
break through the floodgates of your thoughts.
When these barriers of the mind are freed
you'll see my heart is truly yours.
When the chains of these doors are loosed
you'll come and sit here at my feet
combing your curls free in the breeze
that shall intoxicate us with its scent.

The Breeze

The breeze breathed its gentle lyrics
in the ear of the violet, shyly hiding;
it sang softly but incessantly until
that retiring blossom opened wide.

Tomorrow

Don't think you'll ever be perfect.
Nothing can and no one ever will be
as perfect as you imagine
– neither man, woman, nor word.

Because perfection, so I've heard,
is always as far from you as tomorrow:
your feelings, thoughts and efforts
– all the steps you take towards perfection –
wait for tomorrow to happen.

Cycles

The wheel keeps revolving in relentless circles
like a teacher bound by his board.
The dark night keeps brooding despite the bright moonshine
casting shafts of light on the road.
But though the heart keeps beating and cannot be stopped,
the mind can leap upwards, beyond mere hope –
you long for the home that craves your return,
but your soul can't be tied to such cycles.

Anemone

We've reached the end of winter.
I picked a wild anemone,
and tried to graft it
to a stubborn oleander.
Might a new plant blossom?
Might a home-grown anemone
bloom from this unlikely union?

Longing to Fly

Although you're rooted to your feet
you long for the sky;
although you're sister to the dust
you yearn to fly high.

Your feelings spill, surge and overflow,
youthful and pure:
the summons of the sun is near –
step into its sphere!

The Blossom

The prayer of the flower was answered.

After giving up its colour, leaving a complexion jaded,
after giving up its fragrance, with a scent that had faded,
after letting all its petals drop down one by one – at last
it turned into a tender fruit: one of the finest.

Would that our lives might blossom with such taste.

The Prayer of the Tree

That hapless tree that sat through all the winter months out there
naked in the snow and ice, its shivering branches bare,
broken, wind-torn, bleak and dreary,
bent by the changing seasons, weary,
has finally had an answer to its prayer.
See how the kind Creator full of loving care
has decked it in new garments, fresh and rare!
Have you seen how green it is at last, how finely dressed, how fair?

Spring

One season is over and another come;
new days are with us, old ones gone.
In the previous garden, all the buds died –
some thoughtless fool had tied them by the neck
and broken all their stems – everything's wasted.
But trees stood upright still despite being blasted,
and the air in that plot was promise-filled
with everyone believing lies and whispers,
fairy tales about dry branches growing at will,
and despite being rootless, blooming still.

And all the while another voice was calling:
Go tell about the gardener and new garden!
Go spread the word across the field and meadow,
stir the deep waters, wake the lazy springs
shake the violets from their drowsy sleep
and break the boughs that offer futile hopes!
Say: One season's passed, another summons!
The time of jealousy and tears has gone;
the reign of envy's past and all that was.
The hour of fruition's come at last!

I dreamed once of a woman giving birth
to a baby in the middle of the street,
and as soon as the little one was born
she bent her head and gently kissed its feet.
And I heard that voice then, in the middle of the night
I heard that call which took root in my heart,
filling me with joy and delight.
For at the sound, instead of gold,
I felt my ears were hung with verdant leaves,
green pendants dangling down in silken folds
brushing away my tears and griefs.

Look how they meet and mingle together,
voice and glance melting into each other,
look how the limpid waters ripple and fuse
as heart links to heart at this glad news,

and see the seeds sprout like tiny green lights
in secret rows under cover of night!
So tell about the gardener and new garden!
Go spread the word in field and meadow,
stir the deep waters, wake the lazy springs
shake the violets from their drowsy sleep
and break the boughs that offer futile hopes, singing:
Come! One season's passed, another summons!

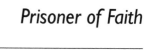

Prisoner of Faith

The Imaginary Garden

There was once a woman
green as the spring,
who planted her hands in a garden.
And another woman,
red as her heart
who plucked light from the bars of a prison.
And now here I am
with my own patch of soil,
growing a garden
in this small cell,
with poppies of love for each pane.

You need just one flower –
that's all it takes –
to open the windows of sight.
A single verse
is quite enough
to illumine the eyes with light.

So I'll tie my bags to the foot of the breeze
and soar high up to the top of the trees
in my garden that grows inside.
And I'll spread wings to reach you
and soar high to teach you
how windows can open wide.
You don't need much:
one poppy is all
it takes to be open to love.
One verse is sufficient
to fill the eyes
with that shining beams from above.

Place of Peril

What are they doing to us in this perilous place,
this prison of loss?
But what can they do to a handful of dust
in the middle of chaos?

If they cut open our veins, red tulips will blush
like blood in the fields.
If they padlock our lips, the mouths of a thousand
spring buds are unsealed.

If they daub us with mud, the dead will arise
to judge their crime.
If they shatter the water jug, spill the cup,
the world floods with our wine.

If they kick in our heads, they crown our brows
with an azure dome.
If they press thorns on our temples, the breath of Jesus
resuscitates the tomb.

If they dig pits at our feet or throw us in wells
Joseph's beauty becomes renowned.
There is nothing to fear in their tempests or storms
while the seas are Noah's own.

Why would we care for cracked earthenware
with precious gems at hand?
As soon as they chain down our feet, they free
the albatross of the mind!

Bar the road to the old and a thousand youths
clamour at the gates;
if this perilous place is so filled with wonders
they'll long to join the feast.

Always With Me

Why is it that despite its reels and shakes
the topsy-turvy world here cannot cause
this throbbing heart of mine to ache?

Why is it that despite the siren's shrill of fear
its anguish cannot reach the boundaries
of my blood, as I lie here?

Why is it that I'm disinclined even to dream
of violence, and my tongue, normally so sharp,
can say no ill, and thus is rendered dumb?

And how is that despite years in this cell
and all the routine habits of this prison mill
I do not feel that I am really here at all?

You are with me
you are always with me
you are thriving in my heart, alive within me.

If I have not yet died here it is because
they cannot take from me what I shall never lose.

A Tale of Love

When I heard a soft step in my chamber, I knew it was you;
I cast off the veil and dressed in rich robes of ecstasy.

And as each breath I drew brought me nearer reunion with you,
I found proof of your presence tossed over the paths of ecstasy.

The bright light of the word so few can understand is yours;
what other face can blind so many that they flee from ecstasy?

The chain that has shaken the earth must surely be yours;
who else can make us call out 'Yea!' in such ecstasy?

You brim from a familiar cup but can this wine really be yours?
Can a pearl break open its own shell through sheer ecstasy?

The passing step that aroused my city could only be yours;
I woke up in love without even a glimpse of your ecstasy!

Tell us, All-seeing One, All-wise, what destiny's ours?
Sit with us, O candle of the world, at the banquet of ecstasy!

Tell us, pure light of our eyes, the tale of love that is ours;
renew and replenish us, Royal One, and restore our ecstasy.

You lifted night's veil so the crown of the dawn must be yours;
you came unannounced and shattered our chains with ecstasy.

Will you lift my despondency too with those bright beams of yours?
Will you pierce this black night and fill me with ecstasy?

Light of All Life

I'll not turn from you, though you cast me aside;
I'll give up my life for a glance from your eyes.

I'll blaze like the stars if you breathe on my light,
pitch my tent on the moon if you pass me one night.

A soft breeze from you cleans the clay of my soul;
being the earth at your feet transmutes me to gold.

This delirium has made me the talk of the town:
one thought of your spring and my whole garden blooms.

But, light of all life, what's made you withdraw?
Abandon me now, and I'm worse than before.

You're the light of the world and time's giver of life;
part your lips an instant and we're shaken by strife.

Blow your trumpet again and we're nothing but dust;
dazed by you each day's a new law for the just.

I rejoice in this kinship, bow my head to this chance;
accept my heart's stone, and it's a jewel at once.

See how my veins thirst for the stroke of the knife
and my eyes yearn to see the light of my life.

The Vast Immensity of My Beloved

I think I must be a tiny fish
and you the limitless ocean,
for how I love you,
O vast immensity!
I think you must be the source
of faith, of truth, of everything that's right,
for how I love your swirling deeps
your blue profundities replete
with corals and with pearls,
O vast immensity!
I love you for increasing endlessly
for spreading wide, mysteriously,
for being the source of growth and life,
O how I love you,
my beloved vast immensity.

Hello Again

Last night, in the midst of unsettled darkness,
I found myself at the axis of the earth for a moment,
holding it taut between my outstretched arms.
And as I struggled to keep those frozen poles apart,
I saw I could palpate these icy limbs
and melt them wondrously between my two hot palms.
So there I stood on the summit of the loftiest peak:
a simple woman, glowing with love again,
ready to salute the world once more.

Not Too Far Off

Though they still lie smothered,
still lie wrapped in cobwebs,
still slumbering the night out,
these souls yearn for the sun.
Their hearts cry out for the daylight,
even as they rage against the black-out,
longing for the warmth of a glance,
for the brightness of a bending gaze,
for the balm of healing hands after lights out.
The day will come when the young among them
will flee from this jungle darkness
and will run out to embrace the sun.

That day's not too far off.

Blessedness

Blessed is the seed whose shoots grew green,
blessed the offshoot burgeoning to a branch,
blessed the branch that brings forth early blooms,
blessed those patient blossoms that bear fruit,
and blessed the fruits containing yet more seeds.
How blessed the seeds, the offshoots, and the boughs,
the branches, and the blossoms too, how truly blessed!
Dear God! What blessings showered upon this world!

Waterfall

I am possessed of love from head to foot,
submerged and drowned beneath the flood,
the mighty waterfall of you.

Let me tell of this unending inundation,
share these showers coursing through my blood,
this tumbling cataract of you.

The furnace of scorched suffering dissolves
and burning adversities are quenched
by a drop of love from you.

Even without seeing any signs, I sense
the perfume of your breath, am drenched
in the compassionate depths of you.

Do not abandon me to myself,
sweet swelling freshness.
Stay, and fill my soul,
eternal waterfall.

Knowing

Like a zephyr at the hour of dawn,
like a morning breeze you roused me.
One breath from you and up I leapt
to follow where you'd passed me.

I walked – such ecstasy! – step after step,
ran even! But you'd taken flight,
leaving me leaden, loaded, chained,
while you melted into the light.

When your bright day reigns at last
love will surely triumph over fears.
Only then shall I know at last
what true freedom is from tears.

Fire

They set fire to all you had;
each flame transformed
into a bright anemone of blood.
They pierced you through and shot
each arrow owned by old Farhad.
But when the sweet juice stained
the ground, it flowed from Shirin's vein.

Fariba

Fariba Kamalabadi was arrested, imprisoned and condemned to twenty years imprisonment together with Mahvash Sabet and five other Bahá'ís because of her membership on the Yaran. During the early years of their incarceration they were in the same cell. They have been separated since 2011.

Stay Near Me

To my dear Fariba

How can I,
without your mirror,
know who I rightly am?
Stay near that we may be united
and forever remain.

Every morning
I feel myself melting,
flowing and coming alive,
as I dive in the crystal clear springs
of your heart's waves.

Every evening
I am drained dry
deprived of your glowing rays,
and the colours that gleam brightly
in your sweet eyes.

In my solitude
I find myself smiling
at the memory of your happiness,
and my tears are grafted to your laughter
in this loneliness.

Stay near me,
dear soul, so pure,
so candid and so true,
for how can I know myself again
deprived of the sight of you?

Deep in My Heart

You spread calm wings over the turbulence,
the frenzy boiling deep within my heart.
But was my breath too hot for you at last,
was it too intense down there?
I sometimes wonder if you've cast away
our fellowship, shed our affinities. Oh, don't
forget this friendship, for alas, without you
I am bereft, dear one, I swear.
I am a wanderer adrift in this unthinking crowd,
a stranger groping for a way among the blind.
No one here can touch me to the quick like you.
None comes as near to me as you, none can find,
as you did, my vein of throbbing pride.
But you're far from me now, you've floated off,
attracted to the mystic realms on high.
I see you soaring in solitude to worlds beyond,
where foolish whims like mine can never aspire.
Tell me, dear one, what you're doing there?

Prostration

I pick a bunch of flowers
from the carpet in our home
and you pluck a branch of light
from the distant sun.
I choose to be prostrated,
kiss the earth on which I lie;
you rise still higher in stature
till you touch the Milky Way.

A Distant Remembrance

It's one of those days
when my jungle-green eyes
have turned towards the gaze
of the bright azure skies
and I've stretched out both arms
to reach the warm hands
of the generous sun.

Some time has passed
since I was first incarcerated
in this labyrinthine place,
but one memory still lingers
in the heart of the jungle;
a distant remembrance remains
    as I recall:
your shining eyes, your kind, warm hands,
    and that is all.

To Fariba Kamalabadi

O my companion in the cage! How many cruelties we saw together;
how many favours too and blessings in our isolation.

Even in the face of death, our lips were graced by the smile of longing.
Even as we ran from place to place, we anticipated our eternal home.

The hunter overturned the little hearth we built, our little household;
how cruelly he turned our lives and our small comforts upside down.

The cocoon that we had built together, you and I, was tight and tiny
but quite large enough to house a growing butterfly.

They tied your wings to mine, feather to feather,
and you rested your head beside mine every night.

The bitter cold of Dey that month and our terror of the cruel storm
have faded now, to my surprise, and are quite forgotten.

A long time has passed since the hand of tyranny was first raised
against us,
a long time since this blazing furnace opened on our heads to burn us.

A long time has passed since those Yaran meetings of ours,
a long time since we dressed in robes of faith and radiant acquiescence.

In this perilous plight we've given ourselves up for lost a hundred times.
We have flung all our clothes away as we passed by the tavern.

In the heart of this battlefield we have sealed our end a thousand times,
intoxicated by the joyous memory of the Beloved of all hearts.

In the end we will forget these pangs of separation for they'll be
no more.
The bane of this cup which it's been our lot to drink will be no more.

A hundred stones have bruised our breasts and lips, but they are sealed;
all the false charges which were hurled against us shall melt away.

O my companion in the cage! May your cup fill with faith
and your breast brim with the remembrance of His loved ones.

May your land flourish, your heart leap in ecstasy forever,
and your memory redound with the jubilation of the people of Iran.

Other Dedications

The Wall

Offered to my sister

A bird flew by
high in the sky
far above these towering and oppressive walls
interlocked and woven with barbed wires.
A bird flew by
high in the sky
beyond my reach.
And I, on the other side of this wall
saw that calm and easy flight
saw the high blue sky
and that pure lofty moving thing
and recognized your eyes
engraved there in the heart of the clouds.
And I saluted the blue sky then and the clouds and the high-flying bird
and your heart-warming eyes were gazing down at me from the clouds.
Look!
See how in the middle of my anguish and my pain
                              even so
the highest realms of the sky and freedom still remain!
And I marvel at these heights above us,
at the eternal sky hanging over us,
at the vast distances and lights shining on us,
and the winds that blow over these wretched walls.
Yes, these walls are truly wretched, worthless, pointless.
for you are here inspite of them,
and I am sitting right beside you,
as I meditate on the heights
of the sky,
and the speed
of the winds.
And all the while you're with me
and I'm sitting right beside you.

Home

On the occasion of the birthday anniversary of my husband, Siyavash

Home was so beautiful!
The tree, bird-filled,
wild with yellow canaries
warbling their melodies,
singing their dawn prayers;
and the purple lilacs
drenching the wall with perfume;
and the vines, grape-filled,
drooping from the trellis.

And every day
beneath its shade
I would drink from that heart-juice,
with the garden rippling round me
like mercury in the sun.

And every morning
I would open the windows, crying –
Greetings to the earth!
Good day to the air!
Hello to the neighbour's sweet briar!

The breeze was cool with your breath
and you were in every corner, fragrant:
the waft of a curtain, the lilt of a song.
And you were in every step of this home:
the tempo of a tune, the verse of a poem.

It was full of splendour and delight,
with everyone busy, a home of joy;
even the little ones were happy
in their room brimming with toys.

Your prayers tasted of eternity there:
filled with faith, winged with wonder.
We were all in love with the rain there:
the swaying of trees, the music of praise.
We were delirious with nearness down by the sea shore,
filled with the ecstasy of that immense presence.

Home was beautiful
with everyone busy doing things.
Your prayers there tasted of eternity.

The Past

It's dawn and the sound of the *azan*
is heard by those awake as well as those asleep.
I close my eyes
but I cannot doze off again.
The prison cells are silent all around us
and the cool breeze carries me back to my childhood.
Summer time on the sunbaked roof of the house.
the sky is a clean black board
covered with brilliant stars
and the beds are cool
as the earthenware pots and sweet melons of *Gorab*.
Father always sleeps with his arms across his forehead.
Mother cradles my little brother Hormoz in her embrace.
And there's my younger sister
and my mother's brother Houshang
and further away my darling grandmother
whose love has taken root in the deepest recesses of my life.

My father was all power and my mother
a full-length mirror of love and benevolence.
I never knew how my father learned the secrets of upright living
                                    from the lofty cypress.
I never found out in which school my mother learned the lessons
                                    of hope and joy.
He walked tall as the mountain top and taught trees
to hold their heads up just as high, reciting poems
as tempestuous as the one and as calm as the other.
She overflowed with faith, was fearless;
no clamour, no uproar ever disturbed her.

We knew that father would always be there, would always be strong;
we knew that he could do anything once he decided to do it.
The only thing he failed to do was to prevent death when it came.
Like the waves in a storm
he could never be idle
was forever at it, coming, going,
always finding a way,
the shorter the better.

Mother was all enthusiasm, all eagerness;
she was in love with light
and had no complications.
Mother knew the secret ways of water and green fields;
she knew the hidden arts of kindness.
She adored gardens and flowerbeds,
loved happiness and laughter.
With a handful of wheat she could cook a whole loaf of bread,
and with its fragrant freshness could conquer an entire country.
When she was able to share her loaf with the neighbour she was happy.
In her eyes, everything in life should be simple:
the house was simple, the garden simple;
the table was simple and so were sorrows and joys.
Mother's umbrella was simple, her perfume was simple,
and kindness was the simplest of all.
But her love was deep and her pains too
and her friendship was as deep as it was true.

Father was the enemy of darkness;
he longed to illumine the crooked paths and narrow ways.
He was active and always in motion.
His brow shone as bright as the day.
And when the house lights went on at night
all our relationships were clear.
All selfish motives and muddled intentions
were exposed, in the open, without fear.
My father loved people;
he could distinguish good wheat from chaff
and was always happy to put bread on peoples' tables,
a friend to all and open-hearted towards everyone.

Mother was always thinking of the migration of swallows.
She was a running river, a sea rippling with waves;
she was like a rain cloud and a field in spring:
always over-flowing, never stagnant.

Now mother is alone and writes letters to father.
He is preparing a different life for us.
'You can have whatever you want,' he tells us,
'If you work for it. That's the law of life.'

He wanted a different life and succeeded
in achieving his aims. He came back then
and took us away with him.
And my mother had already prepared everything to go.
She was weary of the narrow cistern;
she was like a fish leaping towards the ocean.

I smell the fresh brewed tea. Alas!
I don't want any breakfast.
Oh guard, can't you let me return
to that flat roof of sunbaked bricks
and the old earthenware jug of water
to the smell of the sweet melon of *Gorab*
and the cool bedding,
to the star-studded sky
and my gentle grandmother,
to my beloved little sister Parivash
and my brother.
I want to return to the arms of my mother
under the shadow of my father's protection.

I dreamt of her last night.

Happy Day

To dear Sami – Happy Birthday

The day when this plant, crowned with blooms,
will finally raise its shaking head above the wall,

The day when the dancing narcissus will stir
and wake the garden flowers, one and all,

The day when these pains recede, these fevers
break so the paroxysms are relieved for all,

The day when no one is punished for the sake
of her beliefs or subjected to another's will,

The day when mothers won't be thrown in prison
or abandon their children in ways so cruel,

The day when persecution and detention cease
and this oppressive siege comes to a final end:

That day you will be decked in honour and in pride
for you too have played your part in this crusade.

Let Time Slow Down

Written during the last hours of the life of my friend Naheed Ayadi, in memory of the many journeys and long distances we travelled together in the service of the Cause

Let time slow down.
With no chance of a last meeting
that dear one is gradually drifting.
She has no strength for embracing
and no hope of another greeting.
Her soul pines to be flying,
but though she's sick of her ailing
don't let her bright eyes be closing
too soon. Let time slow down.

I wish these prison bars would break,
before it's too late to see her again.
I wish I could glimpse her kindly face,
hear her uplifting laughter once again,
I yearn to catch sight of her beaming smile
just one more time, just one last?
But her soul is poised for the future again
while my heart still dwells on the past.
I conjure the memory our beginnings again
even as she steadily nears her end –
Oh! too soon. Let time slow down.

If only the imprint of your smile, dear one,
could linger on the face of every flower;
if only your exhilarating glance, dear one,
could bloom with the narcissus every year;
if only your compassionate heart, dear one,
could have taught more souls to love like you;
if only your captivating tenderness, dear one,
could have restored the world's courtesy anew.
How I miss hearing your prayers each night
and the echo of your chant at first light.

Let time slow down.
Don't close your eyes just yet;
I'm still awake and wait here
for the rising of the sun.
The hope of seeing you again, kind one,
turns night to day in this dark prison.
Let time slow down.
Don't close your eyes just yet;
I'm still awake and wait here
for the rising of the sun.

Mother

On the occasion of the 10th anniversary of the passing of my dearest mother, Ashraf

A chained hand can't command the words to tell your tale,
nor a tired heart woo the bride of poetry in your name.
My house is all in ruins, the porch has crumbled down,
but this broken one can't make repairs, even for your sake.
There's no breath left in me, no language any more, yet see
how I use this excuse to measure loss across the years.
Since you went, I've been mourning, friendless and forlorn;
look how the world goes by without you near me any more.
Each dawn, I look for you as soon as I open my eyes
but how can a cistern hold the moon's full shine?
Once you set your earthly life aside to be pure spirit
you broke that shell, and what a pearl you left behind!
Before I came here, you'd lived in this cage yourself
and but for you, I'd never find the patience to remain.
Don't speak to me of kinship: where am I? Where you?
How can a piece of gravel be compared to a hidden gem?
I long for your dignity, who are the noblest of the wise,
for I'd have no higher station than yours in men's eyes.

To My Dearest Violette

A limpid river running to the sea,
a mountain lifted to the sky so bright,
a vista open towards distant lands,
a branch that reaches for the light:
you have lived well, O fortunate one!

Companion of that crimson-petalled rose,
close to the moon and kindred of the stars,
a slave to service, all your life in bonds,
worthy of countless honours and of praise:
you have lived well, O fortunate one!

A being symbolised by love alone
whose lips sung all the melodies of love
with fervour and with wit renowned by all,
alive to the immortality of love:
you have lived well, O fortunate one!

Your enthusiasm causes seas to surge;
your devotion compels clouds to weep.
Purity and trust is what you manifest,
and in our hearts you beat the pulse:
you have lived well, O fortunate one!

You are a seed from the first shoots of green
fervent with the first heard melodies;
you are a pearl of rare and luminous sheen
drawn from out of those early treasuries:
you have lived well, O fortunate one!

Child of compassion and of generosity,
companion of the consort and true confidante,
helpmeet of the one who shared the throne
and now my intercessor and my friend:
you have lived well, O fortunate one!

Notes on the Poems

From Evin to Raja'i Shahr

'*twenty-eighth of Sha'ban*': Saturday 12 June 2010. The day of the trial and conviction of the seven members of the Yaran.

'*The fire of judgement must have burned so fiercely in Tabriz*': a reference to the martyrdom of the Báb in the city of Tabriz in July 1850.

The Friends

A reference to the Yaran.

The Perfume of Poetry

'*the spring of your kind hand*': Fariba Kamalabadi is named in the original poem; she is the other member of the Yaran condemned with Mahvash and, before they were separated in January 2012, imprisoned with her.

'*the warrant*': 'The death warrant' in the original.

Billows of Smoke

'*a puff of a single Zar*': a popular brand of cigarette in Tehran.

Times Gone By

'*Farhad, Shirin and their eternal love stories*': one of the most celebrated love stories in the annals of Persian literature. Farhad was a leader in the army of Kavoos, one of the Kings of ancient Persia, and Shirin was his sweetheart.

Remember Me

'*O servant of that mighty manifestation*': 'Abdu'l-Bahá
'*that One*': Bahá'u'lláh, Founder of the Bahá'í Faith

The Imaginary Garden

'There was once a woman': Reference to the poem *Reborn* by Forough Farokhzad, who died in 1967 and has become an icon of women's freedom in contemporary Iran: 'In the garden I plant my hands/ I know I shall grow, I know'

'and another woman': Ṭáhirih (Qurratu'l-'Ayn), an early Bábí poet and proponent of religious reform in Iran, who cast aside the veil and was strangled for her beliefs in an abandoned orchard, in 1852.

Fire

'Farhad' and *'Shirin'*: see above, *Times Gone By*.

To Fariba Kamalabadi

'The bitter cold of Dey': The 10th month of the Iranian calendar, between December and January, marking the start of winter.

The Past

'azan': The call to dawn prayer.

'Gorab': A high plateau at 8,000 feet altitude in Kermanshah, famous for melons and cucumbers.

Milton Keynes UK
Ingram Content Group UK Ltd.
UKHW040642061023
430068UK00001B/50